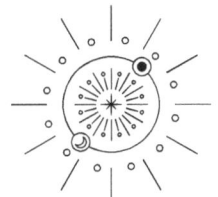

"Spring is the time of plans and projects. It is a season of renewal, where the earth awakens, flowers bloom, and everything feels alive with possibility. Just as nature transforms, so can we - shedding the old, embracing new growth, and stepping forward with fresh energy and hope."

Inspired by Leo Tolstoy

Dedicated to
Victoria. Thank you for helping me
create a new beginning.
Cugs

Tee

www.TeannaTaylor.com

© Teanna Taylor 2025 All Rights Reserved

First Edition 2025
Published by Teanna Taylor Publishing

No part of this book may be copied or reproduced in any format, by any means, electronic or otherwise, without prior consent from the copyright owner and publisher.

This workbook is created and published for informational purposes only. It is not intended to be a substitute for professional medical advice and should not be relied on as health or personal advice. Always seek the guidance of your doctor or other qualified health professional with any questions you may have regarding your health or a medical condition.

SPRING
Sowing the Seeds of Intention

**Cosmic Energy of:
Growth, New Beginnings, Potential, and Planting.**

This workbook aims to guide you in setting meaningful intentions and planting the seeds of your dreams.

It accompanies the book 'Unclock Your Cosmic Flow'

How To Use This Workbook

This workbook is designed to accompany the book
Unlock Your Cosmic Flow
Which covers manifesting in line with the Cosmic Energy of the seasons in much more detail.

This workbook contains practical exercises, support and guidance to help you manifest your dreams while aligning with the Cosmic Energy of Spring.

There are weekly tasks, some daily, structured to be manageable and not overwhelming or time-consuming - remember...

> *...the art of manifesting with Cosmic Flow is to set your intention, feel it, act on it, and let it go.*

Tee

Each full moon has a bespoke ritual, with more in-depth exercises, to boost personal energy aligned with that of the Cosmos. These pages are coloured grey for ease of finding.

Further guidance and support are available online on social media with affirmations, top tips, and, of course, my meditations.

Follow the workbook week by week—the dates are at the top of each new week, which starts on a Friday, not a Monday, so you have the weekend to do the exercises. If you miss a day or a week, just let it flow and catch up if you can. But try to stay on track with the full moons, for those are your natural energy boosts.

Key

General Information and Instructions

The Science Behind the Exercise

Exercise Start

Things You Will Need

Meditation On Line
www. TeannaTaylor.com

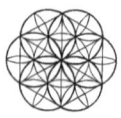

Thursday, 20th March 2025 - Vernal Equinox   11
- Find Your Soul Purpose
- Where Are You Now - Life Wheel
- Spring Check-In
- Meditation Online - 'Cosmic Flow Connection - Spring'

- **Friday, 21st March - Embracing New Beginnings**   25
- Create New Intentions and Action Plan
- Create a Sacred Space

Friday, 28th March - Aligning with Nature's Rhythms   39
- Create a Vision Board

Friday, 4th April - Surrending to Springs Flow   43
- Daily Morning Surrender
- Creating Affirmations

Friday, 11th April - Pink Full Moon   45
- Self Love Quiz
- Practice Self Love
- Add Pink to your Sacred Space
- Meditation online - 'Pink Moon Self Love'

Friday, 18th April - Cultivating Gratitude   54
- Create a Grateful Jar

Friday, 25th April - Planting the Seeds of Dreams   56
- Planting Seeds Letter to Self

Friday, 2nd May - Grounding and Connection   58
- Daily Barefoot Grounding and Rooting

Friday, 9th May - Planting Affirmations for the Future   59
- Create Affirmations

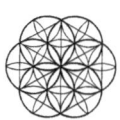

Dates

Sunday, 11th May - Flower Full Moon   61
- Full Moon Release and Burn Ritual
- Plant Seeds of Abundance
- Add Fresh Flowers to your Sacred Space
- Meditation online - 'Seeds of Dreams'

Friday, 16th May - Awakening Potential   65
- Create a Daily Nature Walk

Friday, 23rd May - Rebirth of Self   69
- Create an Action Plan

Friday, 30th May - Visualising Success   70
- Visualisation - Using Senses

Friday, 6th June - Organising Thoughts   72
- Create a Mind Map

Tuesday, 10th June - Strawberry Full Moon   74
- Self Assessment Quiz
- Reframing Limiting Beliefs and Creating an Action Plan
- Add something Red to your Sacred Space
- Meditation online - 'Strawberry Moon Nurturing Your Intentions'

Friday, 13th June - Refining Intentions   81
- Intention Review

Friday, 20th June - Reflection   87
- Grateful Jar Review
- Life Wheel Reflection
- Celebration of Small Wins

Introduction

Spring is a season of 'Awakening' - a time when the natural world bursts into life after the stillness of winter. Flowers bloom, seeds sprout, and animals emerge from hibernation. The earth vibrates with energy, fertility, and potential. This season carries a unique vitality that invites renewal and growth, symbolising fresh beginnings. Just as the soil prepares to nurture new life, we, too, can embrace this opportunity for transformation.

The power of spring for manifestation is not just poetic; it is backed by neuroscience. When we set intentions during a season characterised by growth and renewal, our brains are more receptive to creating new neural pathways. This is partly due to a natural surge in dopamine, the "feel-good" neurotransmitter, which plays a crucial role in motivation and goal achievement.

Dopamine levels rise when we set clear intentions and take action, particularly during a season that encourages growth. This neurotransmitter enhances focus and drive, making it easier to pursue our goals. By setting small, achievable tasks - like organising a room or starting a new habit - we stimulate dopamine release, reinforcing our momentum and enthusiasm.

Spring also boosts serotonin levels, the neurotransmitter linked to mood regulation and emotional well-being. The increased exposure to sunlight and longer daylight hours naturally elevates serotonin, improving our mood, energy levels, and motivation. This seasonal uplift aligns our minds and bodies for growth, making it the perfect time to plant the seeds of our dreams.

Spring is more than just a season; it is a powerful reminder of the cycles of life, renewal, and infinite possibility. By consciously aligning with this energy, we can manifest our dreams with greater ease and joy. Just as nature awakens, our aspirations can blossom and thrive.

Cosmic Flow Manifesto

I invite you to trust the Cosmic rhythm and embrace the cyclical journey by signing your personal manifesto – a promise to yourself. Feel free to modify it to reflect your beliefs.

My Manifesto for Living in Harmony with Cosmic Flow

I commit to aligning with the natural rhythms of the Cosmos, recognising that life flows in cycles of birth, growth, decay, and renewal. I embrace each season and moment, balancing action with rest and trusting in divine timing.

I pledge to treat all beings with kindness, celebrating our interconnectedness. I practice gratitude for every experience, understanding that challenges are teachers. I let go of what no longer serves me, trusting that new growth will come.

Above all, I dedicate myself to love, balance, and presence. I will move with the Cosmos, embracing every cycle as part of my journey.

So it is, and so it shall be.

Sign _____   Date _____

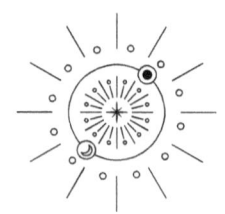

"Your purpose in life is to find your purpose and give your whole heart and soul to it."

Buddha

Welcome to Spring!
Vernal Equinox Ritual
Thursday 20th March 2025

The Spring Equinox, often referred to as the Vernal Equinox, marks the official arrival of spring in the Northern Hemisphere, typically occurring between March 19th and 21st. This moment occurs as the Sun gracefully crosses the celestial equator, resulting in nearly equal hours of daylight and darkness across the globe. This is when Cosmic Energy starts its new cycle and starts to grow in strength for the Northern Hemisphere.

The term "equinox" is derived from the Latin phrase meaning "equal night," which signifies that day and night stretch to approximately 12 hours during this time.

This seasonal shift not only brings longer, sun-drenched days but also awakens the world around us, breathing life into the world and ushering in a time of renewal and growth. In contrast, the Southern Hemisphere experiences the Autumn Equinox, a time that signals the onset of fall and the gathering in of nature's bounty.

The equinox is a powerful start to new Cosmic energy, an energy of new beginnings and transformation. It is an ideal moment for setting intentions, purifying personal energies, and embracing personal renewal. The delicate balance between light and darkness serves as a poignant reminder of harmony in life, encouraging introspection and alignment with the ever-changing rhythms of nature.

Take stock of where you are now

Many people miss out on this review stage, but knowing where you are now and where you would like to head is crucial before you set any intentions. So, ask yourself:

- Do I know my soul purpose?
- Do I know where I am now?
- Do I know what direction I am going?
- Do I know what I want to manifest?
- Do I know what intentions to set to achieve this?

If the answer to any of these is no, then the next excercises can help, as knowing the answers to some of these, at least, can give you the direction in life so many have not reached, but remember not to set rigid limits or goals; it is more about heading in a direction and then aligning your energy and then 'trust and flow' that the outcome will appear. Also, when you set limits, that is all you will reach - don't set a limit, and you will go further.

Practical Exercises
Take Stock of Where You Are Now
Find Your Soul Purpose
Life Balance Wheel
Spring Check-In

Meditation
Listen to the "Cosmic Flow Connection - Spring" meditation.

Find Your Soul Purpose

I have found that the Ikigai exercise is perfect for this. Ikigai is a Japanese concept that refers to a person's life purpose or reason for being. It is a way of finding joy and fulfilment by aligning your passions, talents, and profession with the world's needs.

I have taught this now for several years with profound results, seeing faces light up as participants discover so much about themselves, – one potent moment was when a tear rolled over the cheeks of a retired lady – who put 'accomplished' in the Ikigai circle with her realising she had not only found her 'Soul Purpose', but she had 'Lived It'.. Such a beautiful moment.

How it works
The Four Large Circles
(A full-size version is overleaf for you to complete and if this is too small to complete you can print out an A4 version on my website.)

1. In the circle on the left -
   'What you are good at'
Write down your skills, talents, and unique abilities – the ones you were born with and the ones you learned and mastered during your personal life, work, or education. Your existing skills, talents, and expertise are essential.

Ask yourself what you know well. Everything you have done with good results until now has potential value.

Extra helpful questions to analyse:

- What do I excel at doing?
- Is there something I want to be among the best at with some more education and experience?
- Which parts of my (current and/or past) job am I good at?
- What am I among the best at within my school/workplace and/or community?

2. In the top circle - "What you love"

Write things you are passionate about, activities that bring you joy, and tasks and topics that motivate you to get out of bed in the morning feeling excited.

You need to ask yourself what fascinates you, what satisfies you, and what you have the most fun doing.

Additional helpful questions to ask yourself:
- What is thrilling to me?
- What could I talk about for hours on end?
- What would I do if I did not have to be concerned about making money and getting paid?
- How would I spend my time on a long holiday or a free weekend?

3. In the circle on the right - "What the world needs"

Note down what your potential clients/community would benefit from but is not accessible to them – or how you can do it better.

What you are offering has to be something needed in the world, so you do not end up putting a lot of your precious time and energy into something nobody wants or needs. Analyse what the market needs that you can provide better than your competition (or at least that offers better value to begin with). Is there anything particular that your potential clients/community are trying to accomplish in their work or lives, and what tasks and problems do they want to solve?

Other questions to ask yourself:

- What issues in my community would I like to help solve?
- What matters in my community that I care about, and what problems affect me emotionally?
- Will some of my work be relevant a decade from now, and whose life will it influence?

4. In the bottom circle - "What I can be paid for"

Write down services, tasks, and niches that may give you the most significant return on your time investment and for which you can get paid more.

We have to pay our bills. No matter what, your Ingki should not keep you up at night wondering how to stay afloat. It would be a shame to, at best, break even from a 'pricey hobby' that takes up your time, money, and emotional resources.

Some other important questions to ask yourself:

- For what work have I already been paid?
- Are other people being paid for this work?
- Am I already making a good living doing what I am doing?
- If not, according to the current market, can I eventually make a good living doing this work?
- Are people willing to pay for what I am doing/selling?

The Four Inner Eclipses

Now, you can move to the inner eclipses and note anything that appears in <u>both</u> the bigger circles.

1. Passion – Combines what you love with what you are good at - so write in here anything which appears in both what you love and what you are good at.

2. Mission – In this eclipse, write down anything which appears in both what you love and what the world needs

3. Vocation – In this eclipse, write down anything which appears in both what the world needs and what you can get paid for.

4. Profession – Finally, in this eclipse, write down anything that appears in what you are good at and what could make you money.

Now, look at all these four eclipses - if anything repeats in <u>ALL FOUR</u> - then you have your Ikigai - Your Life Purpose.

If this diagram is too small you can download an A4 version from my website.

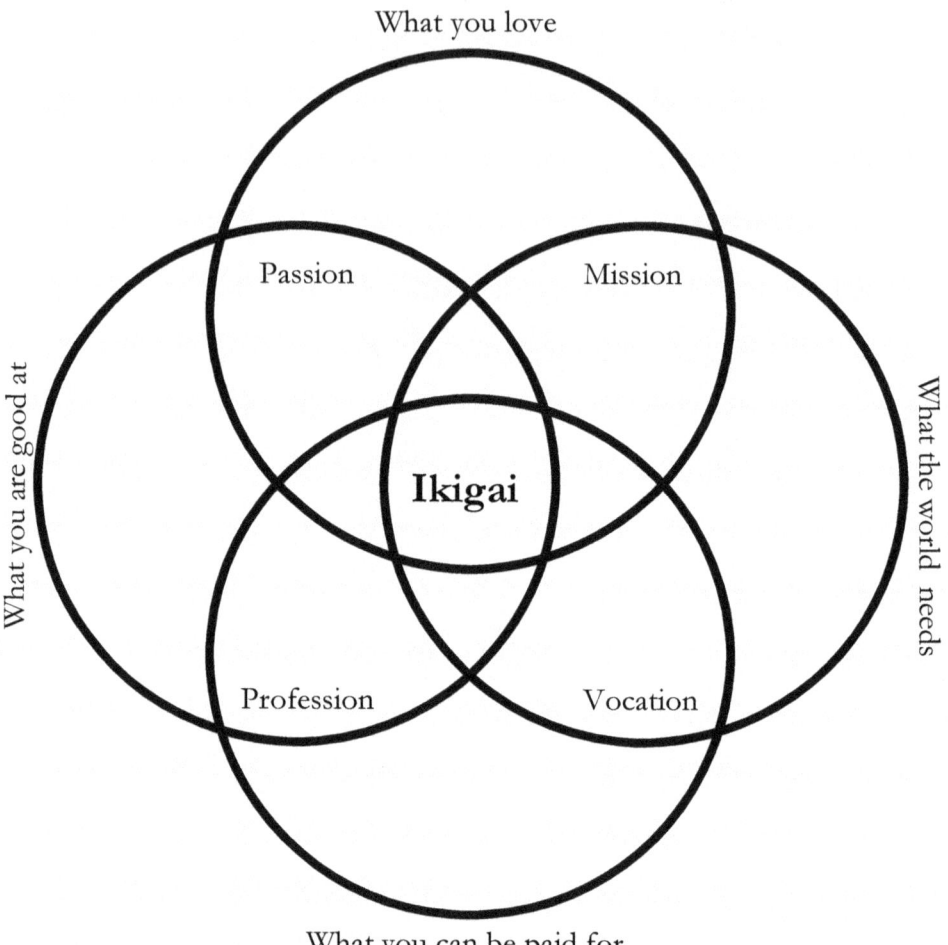

On a personal note, I did this with my daughter at 18 as her soul was not content - and it changed her whole life – from pursuing a degree in Psychology to changing her path completely as 'giving to others via acting or production' was her Ikigai. So, with a deep breath, she changed her university degree – she is trusting and flowing – with her soul alive and brimming with energy. We have no idea where her journey will take her, and its path may change at any moment, but for now, her soul is singing as she listens to its beat!

What if you cannot find your Ikigai

If you did not have anything in all four eclipses - where passion, mission, vocation, and profession overlap - it is entirely okay! It just means you need to explore further.

Here is what you can do:

Reflect on What's Missing
- Look at each of the four sections:
    - What you love
    - What you are good at
    - What the world needs
    - What you can be paid for
- Could you identify which section feels empty or weaker? That is where you need to focus.

Experiment and Explore
- Try new hobbies, volunteer, or take on different roles.
- Learn new skills or deepen existing ones.
- Talk to people in different careers or lifestyles that interest you.

Find Patterns in Your Life
- Think about activities that naturally excite you.
- Please remember past moments when you felt deeply engaged or fulfilled.
- Ask friends or mentors what they think you are great at.

Start with What You Have
- Could you work with that if only two or three sections are filled? For example, if you know what you love and are good at, explore ways to make it worthwhile to the world or monetise it.

Be Open to Change
- Ikigai is not something you find instantly - it evolves.
- Your centre might change as you grow and gain new experiences. - Mine certainly did.

If you did not find your Ikigai, reflect on 'what is missing' below.
If you did find your Ikigai smile - and move on to page 19

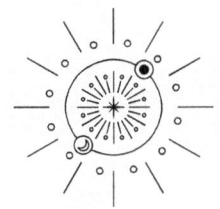

"Balance is not something you find, it's something you create."

Jana Kingsford

Practical Exercise
Create a Life Wheel

This is a powerful self-assessment tool used to evaluate different areas of your life and identify areas for improvement. It visually represents self-awareness and highlights the balance or imbalance across key life areas. Often highlighting areas where you may feel unfulfilled or off balance. Once identified, these areas can help you set meaningful goals and focus. It can also be used to track your progress over time.

How It Works

The 'Life Wheel' is typically a circle divided into segments, each representing a different aspect of life. You rate your satisfaction in each area on a scale from 1 to 10, then plot these scores on the wheel. The result shows whether your life feels balanced or some areas need attention. These out-of-balance areas are usually where your first manifestation intentions come from.

 Common Life Areas in a Life Wheel

Though categories can be customised, a standard version often includes:

- Career and Work – Job satisfaction, growth, and fulfilment.
- Finances – Stability, income, and financial security.
- Health and Wellness – Physical and mental well-being.
- Personal Growth – Learning, self-improvement, and mindset.
- Relationships – Love, friendships, and family connections.
- Spirituality – Inner peace, faith, or connection to a higher purpose.
- Fun and Recreation – Hobbies, leisure, and joy.
- Environment – Living space, work environment, and surroundings.

What to do
- Contemplate each area of life and rate it on a scale of 1 - 10. 1 being completely dissatisfied and 10 being completely content.
- Then, draw a line around the arc or colour in the section from the centre towards the appropriate arc.

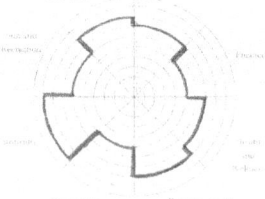

Example

Most people first look to manifest those areas with a low score (closer to the centre) to bring life back into balance.

Life Wheel

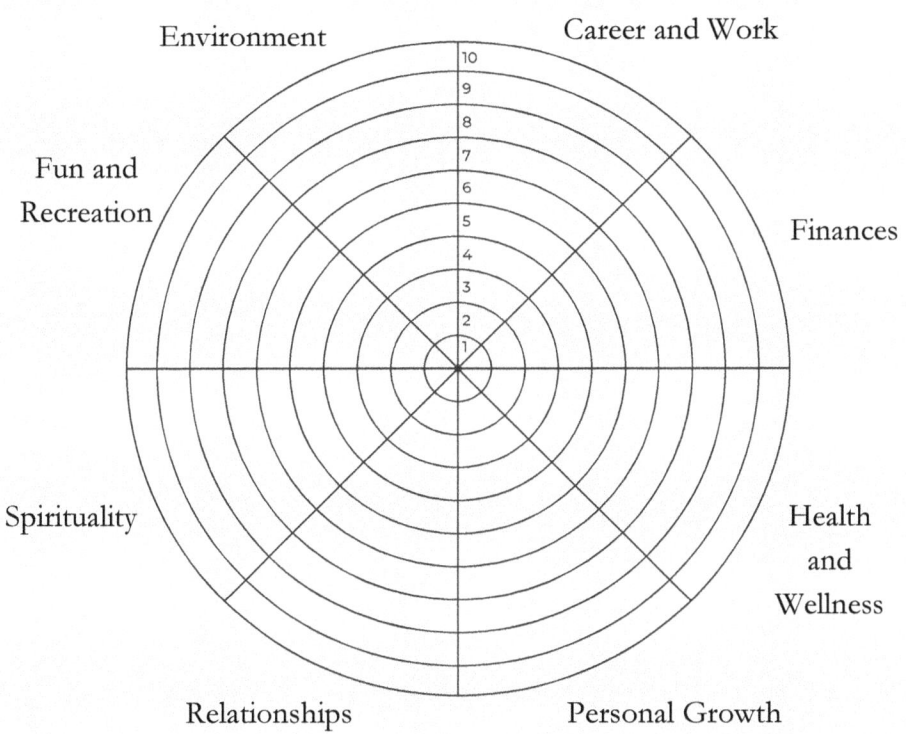

Practical Exercise
Spring Check-in

Use the Life Wheel to help you complete the following check-in. Then, sit with this for 10 minutes per day for this week, and add anything else that comes to mind. This is your subconscious brain linking with Cosmic Flow and bringing more things to the surface.

1. What areas of my life feel ready for growth or renewal?

2. What obstacles or fears are there that might be holding me back from starting fresh?

2. What new ideas, projects, or habits do I want to plant this season?

Friday 21st March 2025

Embracing New Beginnings
Setting Intentions for the Year Ahead

Practical Exercise
Intentions

Using last week's notes, write down 3-4 intentions or goals you want to manifest this year. Break each goal into small, actionable steps. I have included an abstract from the 'Unlock Your Cosmic Flow' book on the following pages as a reminder of how to set meaningful intentions. But go back to the main book for more help if needed. Full details on this whole process are included in that book.

Example:

> **Intention**
> I step into a fulfilling and prosperous career that aligns with my passions, talents, and purpose as a meditation facilitator and author, teaching others the power of meditation and the Cosmos. Opportunities flow to me effortlessly, and I am confident, capable, and ready for this new chapter of success.

Tick off when done   **Steps**

- [✓] Develop a signature style – USP
- [✓] Teach this face-to-face groups and learn more
- [ ] Build my platform and presence
- [✓] Begin my author journey and share my teachings
- [ ] Create income streams and opportunities
- [ ] Gain a book deal and help even more people worldwide

The following is to help you set meaningful intentions.
It is an abstract from
'Unlock Your Cosmic Flow'

*"Intentions matter -
what you send out,
you receive back!"*
Tee

Manifestation involves several key aspects that combine to bring your desires into reality. The first step is having clarity of desire. This means identifying what you want to achieve or attract into your life. Knowing precisely what you want is essential, as it focuses and directs your manifestation process. Let us take the simple desire to manifest a new job. Do not be vague and wish for "a better job." Be specific and write, "I am manifesting a position as a marketing manager at a well-established company where I can apply my skills and grow professionally."

Remember, manifestation is most powerful when rooted in gratitude, alignment, and authenticity. Practice your belief and have faith in it, or, as I like to use 'Trust' and 'Flow' (trust), believe that achieving your goal is possible and align your mindset with this conviction. When you genuinely think your desire is attainable, you begin to take the necessary steps (flow) towards it with confidence and determination.

Intentions, however, should always be positive, set without ego and not aimed to harm anyone or anything. Examples of negative intentions are:

Negative intention examples are:

Control Over Others
Trying to manifest influence over someone's decisions, emotions, or actions go against free will and often lead to toxic relationships.

Material Greed Without Purpose
Manifesting excessive wealth or luxury only for selfish gain, without gratitude or a desire to share abundance can lead to emptiness.

Jealousy and Comparison
Wishing for success to surpass or outshine others rather than for personal fulfilment brings insecurity and dissatisfaction.

Revenge and Harm
Manifesting negative outcomes for someone who wronged you creates a cycle of negativity and often rebounds in unexpected ways.

Fame and Recognition for Ego
Seeking attention and validation from others purely to feed an ego rather than for meaningful contribution, can lead to shallow success.

Desperation and Neediness
Manifesting out of a place of lack or desperation (e.g., "I need this or I'll be miserable") reinforces scarcity and fear.

Instant Gratification
Wanting immediate results without patience, hard work, or responsibility can lead to unsustainable or fleeting success.

Seeking Validation
Manifesting success, beauty, or wealth solely to gain approval from others keeps you trapped in external validation rather than internal fulfilment.

Power and Domination
Wishing to be "better than" or to dominate others through status, influence, or control creates toxic dynamics and attracts conflict.

Dishonest Gain
Hoping for success, wealth, or opportunities through deception, manipulation, or unethical means often leads to long-term consequences.

Avoiding Accountability
Manifesting an escape from problems instead of personal growth and resolution can create a cycle of running from responsibilities.

Wishing for Others to Fail
Hoping competitors, ex-partners, or others struggle to make yourself look better breeds negativity and bad karma.

Superficial Beauty or Attraction
Wanting to manifest physical appearance changes purely for vanity or attention, without self-love, can lead to body image struggles.

Addiction to External Rewards
Manifesting money, fame, or status without emotional or spiritual fulfilment often results in emptiness despite material success.

Lust-Based Relationships
Wanting someone solely for their looks or physical attraction rather than a deep connection leads to shallow or toxic relationships.

"What you think, you create.
What you feel, you attract.
What you imagine, you become."
Unknown

Positive intention examples are:

Personal Growth and Self-Love
Manifesting confidence, self-worth, and emotional resilience helps create a fulfilling life from within.

Abundance and Prosperity for All
Wishing for financial success while also desiring to uplift others ensures that wealth is shared and used for good.

Healing and Positivity
Manifesting good health, peace, and happiness for yourself and others foster a positive environment and attract uplifting energy.

Gratitude and Contentment
Manifesting appreciation for what you already have helps attract even more abundance and joy.

Confidence and Self-Worth
Affirming your own value and believing in yourself opens doors to opportunities and fulfilling experiences.

Forgiveness and Letting Go
Manifesting emotional freedom from past hurts allows you to move forward with peace and positivity.

Supportive and Loving Community
Attracting meaningful friendships and relationships that uplift and inspire you to create a fulfilling life.

Aligned Opportunities
Manifesting career, creative, or life opportunities that match your purpose and skills lead to greater satisfaction.

Joy and Playfulness
Calling in more fun, laughter, and lightheartedness helps create
a balanced and fulfilling life.

Generosity and Giving Back
Manifesting the ability to help others
whether through time, resources, or kindness - creates deeper fulfilment.

Healing from the Past
Releasing old wounds and manifesting emotional or physical
healing allows for a fresh start.

Strength and Resilience
Cultivating the ability to handle challenges with grace and perseverance
ensures long-term success.

Alignment with Your Higher Self
Manifesting clarity and guidance from your inner wisdom leads to
greater purpose and fulfilment.

Creativity and Inspiration
Attracting new ideas, artistic flow, and innovative thinking helps
with personal and professional growth.

Peaceful and Restful Sleep
Manifesting deep, restorative sleep improves overall well-being and energy.

Synchronicity and Divine Timing
Trusting that things will unfold at the right time reduces anxiety
and increases faith in the journey.

Strong Boundaries and Self-Respect
Calling in the confidence to say no to what does not serve you
and yes to what uplifts you.

Karma

Negative intentions come under the universal law of Karma.

Karma is a concept that originated in Hinduism, Buddhism, and Jainism but is now widely understood in many cultures around the world. In simple terms, Karma is the universal law of cause and effect. It suggests that every action—good or bad—has consequences that will eventually come back to the person who performed the action.

Karma works on a simple principle: Positive actions bring positive results, while negative actions bring negative results. If you do good deeds, show kindness, and act with good intentions, you will likely experience positive outcomes, such as happiness, success, or good fortune. Conversely, harmful actions, negative thoughts, or hurtful behaviours can lead to suffering, obstacles, or difficulties in the future.

There are some common misunderstandings about Karma. It is not about punishment or reward. Rather, it is a natural law of balance that helps maintain harmony in the Cosmos. Also, Karma is not instant. According to certain beliefs, manifesting can take time, sometimes even in future lives.

The idea of Karma encourages people to live ethically, responsibly, and compassionately. It promotes the understanding that our actions shape our lives and impact our world. By being aware of Karma, individuals can make conscious choices that create positive outcomes and contribute to the greater good.

Intention

Aligned Actions

Tick off when done

- [ ]
- [ ]
- [ ]
- [ ]
- [ ]
- [ ]
- [ ]
- [ ]
- [ ]
- [ ]
- [ ]
- [ ]

Intention

Aligned Actions

Tick off when done

- [ ]
- [ ]
- [ ]
- [ ]
- [ ]
- [ ]
- [ ]
- [ ]
- [ ]
- [ ]
- [ ]
- [ ]

Intention

Aligned Actions

Tick off when done

- [ ]
- [ ]
- [ ]
- [ ]
- [ ]
- [ ]
- [ ]
- [ ]
- [ ]
- [ ]
- [ ]
- [ ]

Intention

Aligned Actions

Tick off when done

- [ ]
- [ ]
- [ ]
- [ ]
- [ ]
- [ ]
- [ ]
- [ ]
- [ ]
- [ ]
- [ ]
- [ ]

Practical Exercise
Create a sacred space/altar

Creating a sacred space or altar is a deeply personal and meaningful practice that helps cultivate peace, focus, and connection. Whether for meditation, manifestation, or personal reflection, your sacred space should resonate with your energy and intentions.

To begin, find a quiet and peaceful area in your home where you will not be disturbed. It can be a small corner, a shelf, a table, or even a dedicated room. Ideally, it should feel calm and inviting.

Before arranging your space, reflect on what you want it to represent. Some common intentions include healing and self-care, manifestation and abundance, spiritual connection and meditation. You can set the energy by an affirmation, such as:

"May this space be filled with peace, light, and sacred Cosmic energy."

Why this works

Setting a sacred space or altar for manifestation works because it creates a physical and energetic focal point for your intentions. By dedicating a space to your desires, you reinforce their importance in your subconscious mind and align your energy with your goals. Objects like crystals, candles, symbols, or written affirmations serve as tangible reminders of what you are calling into your life, helping to keep your focus clear and unwavering. Additionally, the act of ritual and intention-setting - whether through meditation, prayer, or visualisation - amplifies the emotional and spiritual connection to your desires, making them feel more real and attainable. This process strengthens your belief, raises your vibrational frequency, and aligns you with the energy of what you wish to manifest, ultimately drawing it closer to you.

Creating a sacred space has scientific backing from psychology and neuroscience, too. The Reticular Activating System (RAS) in the brain filters information, helping you notice opportunities aligned with your desires, much like when you start seeing a specific car everywhere after deciding you want one. Additionally, neuroplasticity shows that repeated thoughts and rituals can rewire the brain, reinforcing confidence and motivation. The placebo effect demonstrates how belief alone can influence outcomes, while engaging in rituals reduces stress by lowering cortisol levels, allowing for a clearer, more focused mind.

While a sacred space or altar is not inherently magical, it acts as a powerful psychological anchor, helping to align thoughts, emotions, and actions with desired outcomes, making manifestation more effective.

 Items for Your Sacred Space

To enhance its energy, consider including meaningful items. Such as:

- A light source to represent energy:
    - Candles
    - Fairy lights
    - Himalayan salt lamp

- Natural elements help balance the space:
    - Earth (crystals, stones, flowers)
    - Water (a small bowl of water, shells, or sacred oils)
    - Fire (a candle or incense)
    - Air (feathers, bells, or incense smoke)
    - Spirit (a symbol of your higher self)

Personal items, such as journals, vision boards, or photos of loved ones, can also bring intention and warmth to the space.

- Crystals are often used:
    - Amethyst for peace
    - Clear quartz for clarity
    - Rose quartz for love
    - Selenite for cleansing

Incense, herbs, and essential oils such as sage, palo santo, lavender, and frankincense can be used with sound healing tools like singing bowls, bells, or calming music to enhance the spiritual atmosphere further.

When you arrange your sacred space, please do it with mindfulness and harmony. You might choose a symmetrical layout for balance or a more organic arrangement to reflect creativity and flow. A central object, such as a candle or crystal cluster, can anchor the space's energy. Keeping a small meditation cushion or chair nearby invites regular use and encourages consistency in your practice.

Make it part of your daily routine to benefit from your sacred space. Spend time meditating, journaling, or practicing gratitude. Lighting a candle and taking deep breaths can center your mind and spirit. Your sacred space reflects your inner world, so allow it to evolve as you grow. Keep it personal, meaningful, and aligned with your energy, making it a sanctuary where you can connect, reflect, and find peace.

Even 10 minutes a day will form a habit - and if you find dust in the space, you know you have lost focus. :)

The Science behind habits
Habit formation is rooted in neuroscience and psychology, particularly in how the brain creates and reinforces behaviours through the habit loop—a cycle of cue, routine, and reward identified by researchers like Charles Duhigg. When a behaviour is repeated consistently, it strengthens neural pathways in the basal ganglia, making the action more automatic over time, a process known as neuroplasticity.

Dopamine, a neurotransmitter linked to pleasure and motivation, also plays a key role by reinforcing habits through rewards, increasing the likelihood of repetition. Studies show that forming a new habit typically takes 21 to 66 days, depending on complexity and consistency. By consciously designing cues, attaching positive reinforcement, and staying consistent, individuals can effectively create lasting habits that align with their goals; so a sacred space gives you a tangible place for all your intentions to stay while you work on them.

Friday 28th March 2025

Aligning with Nature's Rhythm

Practical Exercise
Vision Board

Create a vision board to represent your intentions visually.

Vision Board

Creating a vision board is a powerful manifestation tool that helps you visualise and focus on your goals and dreams. It serves as a visual representation of your intentions, helping to align your thoughts, emotions, and actions with what you want to attract into your life. This can also be created around your Life Wheel - see the example on page 42.

Here is how to create a compelling and inspiring vision board:

What you will need

Gather materials that reflect your intentions. You can create either a physical vision board or a digital one, depending on your preference and the resources you have available.

For a Physical Vision Board:
- Cardboard, corkboard, or canvas (any size you prefer)
- Magazines, newspapers, or printed images from the internet
- Scissors and glue or drawing pins (if using a corkboard)
- Markers, pens, or colored pencils for writing affirmations or captions
- Embellishments – Stickers, glitter, or anything that makes it more visually appealing

For a Digital Vision Board:
- Apps: Canva, Pinterest, or PicMonkey
- Find inspirational images on Unsplash, Pexels, or Google Images
- Quotes and Affirmations: Use text tools to add personalised affirmations or print from my website.

Collect Images and Words that Inspire You
- Choose images and words that resonate with your goals and intentions. Look for visuals that evoke the emotions and experiences you want to attract.

 What to Include
- **Pictures:** Images that represent your goals (e.g., a dream house, a happy couple, a fit and healthy person, travel destinations).
- **Words and Phrases:** Positive affirmations, power words, or quotes that inspire you (e.g., "I am abundant," "Love surrounds me," "Healthy and vibrant").
- **Symbols and Numbers** Specific symbols that have personal meaning (e.g., a heart for love, a pound/dollar sign for wealth, specific dates or numbers).
- **Personal Touches:** Include photos or mementos that resonate with your goals (e.g., past achievements, happy memories).

> **Tip**
> Choose images that evoke strong positive emotions.
>
> The more emotionally connected you are to an image, the more powerful it will be in manifesting your desires.

 Arrange and Assemble Your Vision Board

For Physical Vision Boards
- Arrange your images and words on the board before gluing them down. Experiment with different layouts until you find one that feels right.
- You can group images by category (e.g., career, relationships, health) or mix them for a holistic vision.
- You can overlap images for a collage effect, which creates a dynamic and visually appealing board.
- Write affirmations or captions next to images to amplify your intentions (e.g., "I am thriving in my dream career").

For Digital Vision Boards
- Choose a Template: Use Canva or PicMonkey to select a template or create a custom design.
- Add images and arrange them aesthetically.
- Use motivational words, quotes, or affirmations.
- You can save your digital vision board as your desktop or phone wallpaper for daily inspiration.

Manifest With Your Vision Board

Creating a vision board is not enough—you must use its power through intentional practices. Use it as a tool to feel the emotions you wish to evoke and the visions you want to see.

- Spend 5-10 minutes daily looking at your vision board.
- Visualise yourself living the life shown on the board.
- Feel the emotions associated with your dreams—joy, gratitude, excitement, peace.
- Use affirmations while visualising (e.g., "I am grateful for my fulfilling career").

 Manifestation Ritual

Meditate with your vision board nearby, focusing on the images and affirmations. Use gratitude journaling to express thankfulness for your manifestations as if they have already happened.

 Place It Where You Can See It Daily

- For Physical Boards, place your vision board in a space you frequently visit, such as your sacred space, bedroom, office, or meditation area.
- For Digital Boards: Set it as your computer wallpaper or phone background, or create a digital slideshow to revisit daily.
- You can also take a photo of the physical board and add that to your mobiles and computers as screensavers, wallpaper, etc.

 Trust, Let Go, and Take Action

- Believe that the Cosmos is aligning to bring your vision to life. Trust the process.
- Let go of attachment by avoiding obsessing over how and when your manifestations will happen.
- Taking aligned action by aligning your actions with your vision board is a powerful tool but must be paired with intentional actions. Follow inspired ideas and opportunities that come your way.

 Review and Update Periodically

- Review your vision board every 3-6 months to track your progress.
- Celebrate manifestations and replace achieved goals with new ones.
- Update images and affirmations as your desires and goals evolve.

Tips for Creating a Powerful Vision Board

Be Specific and Clear
The more specific your goals, the more effective the vision board.

Include Emotions
Focus on feelings and experiences, not just material objects

Use Positive Language
Ensure all words and affirmations are in the present tense and positive form.

Make It Personal
Choose images and words that resonate deeply with you

Stay Open to Possibilities
Manifestations may come in unexpected ways—be open to receiving them.

It can feel conflicting when asked to 'be specific' yet 'staying open to possibilities'. But you need to do both - in that you need to be specific on the direction you are going - ie towards your Ikigai and how that is going to feel when you get there - but be open to the possibilities on how you will get there - as it might not be as you planned.

So have the goal - but allow it to move and do not put solid stepping stones in place - you have to flow - but just make sure you are flowing in the right direction.

For example you may wish to be a famous actress and intend to go to university and get a degree and then find an agent and get acting jobs, but while at university you get offered a role which propels you into the stardom you wished for. That's flowing!

Example

In the example above, I have used the Life Wheel and the Vision Board tools together, setting my Intentions from the imbalances found in the wheel. I have looked at areas not balanced in the wheel and created a vision board around them to bring them more into balance via my intentions.

Friday 4th April 2025

Surrendering to Spring's Flow

Practical Exercise
Surrender

Use your sacred space and dedicate 10 minutes to a simple surrender ritual each morning.

Sit or stand in silence, close your eyes, and visualise yourself flowing with the natural rhythms of the season, releasing control over what is outside your power.

Practical Exercise
Affirmations

Write down 3/4 affirmations that support your goals and repeat them aloud. Post them where you will see them regularly, such as your bathroom mirror, work desk, on the fridge door, by your kettle or by your plant pots.

> Remember to keep moving forward with your aligned actions

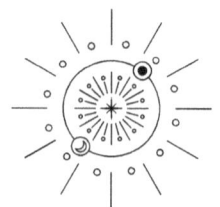

"Every thought we think is creating our future."

Louise Hay

Pink Full Moon
Heart Centered Self Love
11th April 2025

The full moon energy will give your manifestations a boost - so set aside some time this evening to complete the "Heart Centered Self Love Ritual"

Despite its name, the Pink Moon does not appear pink in colour. The name was derived from the early springtime bloom of a pink wildflower called Phlox, commonly known as "moss pink," which is native to North America.

The Pink Moon symbolises renewal, growth, and rebirth, making it a powerful time to embrace new beginnings.

Practical Exercises
Self Love Quiz
Practice Self Love
Add something pink,
ie Pink flowers or Rose Quarts,
to your sacred space/altar

Meditation
Listen to the "Pink Moon Self-Love" meditation

When you start manifesting, you must feel worthy of the manifestation for the right intentions. So, before we begin to plant the seeds of this year's intentions, we must clear our personal energy field/aura/biofield and love ourselves.

Self-love

This is not an ego-driven self-importance or self-obsession form of self-love, which focuses on inflated self-worth or self-admiration that stems from a need for validation, superiority, or constant attention from others. This kind of self-love leads to internal emptiness and a cycle of dependence on external recognition, leaving you feeling unfulfilled despite outward appearances.

When self-love is rooted in ego, it may manifest as:

- **Overinflated Self-Image** - Viewing yourself as superior to others, having a sense of entitlement and disregard for the value of others' feelings or contributions
- **Validation Seeking** - Seeking constant praise, approval, and admiration from others as a form of external validation, with little regard for genuine emotional well-being or inner peace
- **Narcissism** - A sense of entitlement to special treatment or admiration while potentially disregarding the feelings, needs, or rights of others
- **Self-centeredness** - Prioritising your desires above all else, often at the expense of others' well-being or without consideration for the larger community or collective harmony

Healthy self-love, which I am talking about, incorporates compassion for yourself and others, focusing on authenticity, humility, emotional health, growth, and a more profound sense of inner peace. Genuine self-love is about accepting yourself with kindness and understanding, recognising your worth without needing validation. It is about embracing who you are - your strengths, quirks, and imperfections - with kindness and compassion. It means recognising that you deserve care, respect, and understanding from yourself and others.

When you practice self-love, you nurture a positive relationship with yourself, giving yourself the same warmth and encouragement you would offer a dear friend. This might include setting healthy boundaries, treating yourself with patience when mistakes happen, and celebrating your progress, no matter how small.

Self-love helps you build resilience, feel more confident in your journey, and create a foundation for a happier, more balanced life.

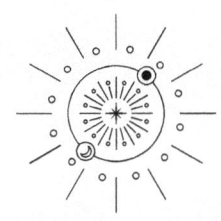

"In essence, self-love is a gentle, ongoing commitment to yourself - a daily reminder that you are valuable, deserving of joy, and capable of growth."

Tee

Practical Exercise
Pink Moon Self-Love Quiz

Discover how connected you are with the nurturing energy of the Pink Moon and explore your self-love journey. There are no right or wrong answers - only insights to help guide you as you embrace the renewing energy of the Pink Moon. Answer each question honestly, then reflect on your responses as you embrace renewal and new beginnings.

1. How do you usually feel when you see the full Pink Moon?
A. Energised and inspired - ready for new beginnings.
B. Calm and reflective - a perfect time for self-care.
C. Indifferent - I rarely notice the moon's phases.
D. Overwhelmed - there is too much pressure to improve.

2. How often do you set aside time for self-reflection or journaling?
A. Daily - It is a must-have part of my routine.
B. A few times a week, I reflect when I need to.
C. Occasionally - mostly when I am feeling stressed.
D. Rarely - I struggle to connect with my inner thoughts.

3. What does self-love mean to you?
A. Embracing my strengths and accepting my imperfections.
B. Nurturing myself with kindness, rest, and self-care.
C. It is something I strive for, but I often struggle with it.
D. I am not sure - I sometimes feel disconnected from the idea.

4. How do you celebrate your achievements?
A. With a personal ritual - lighting a candle or doing a gratitude exercise.
B. By sharing my successes with close friends or family.
C. Quiet acknowledgement without much fanfare.
D. I rarely celebrate, always looking ahead to the next challenge.

5. In times of emotional challenge, what is your go-to strategy?
A. Meditation or mindfulness to reconnect with myself.
B. Talking it out with someone I trust.
C. Distracting myself with hobbies or activities.
D. I feel overwhelmed and lack a clear strategy.

6. How important is the idea of renewal and new beginnings in your life?
A. Extremely - every day is a fresh opportunity to grow.
B. Important - I see change as a natural part of life.
C. Somewhat - I'm still exploring what renewal means to me.
D. Not very - I tend to stick with what is familiar.

7. What comes to mind when you gaze at the Pink Moon?
A. A reminder to nurture my inner garden and let my dreams blossom.
B. A symbol of beauty and self-care, prompting quiet reflection.
C. Just another moon - I do not think much about it.
D. Pressure to live up to ideals of self-love that seem out of reach.

8. Do you feel you allow yourself enough time to rest and recharge?
A. Absolutely - rest is a key part of my self-love practice.
B. Often, although, my schedule gets in the way.
C. I struggle to find balance and often neglect rest.
D. Rarely - I push myself too hard without taking breaks.

9. How connected do you feel to the natural cycles (like the moon's phases)?
A. Very connected - nature's rhythms deeply inspire my growth.
B. Moderately connected - I appreciate them when I can.
C. A little connected - I am aware but not deeply engaged.
D. Not connected - I do not see how they relate to my journey.

10. What do you hope to achieve by embracing the Pink Moon's energy?
A. Greater self-awareness and a deep commitment to self-love.
B. A sense of balance and an appreciation for my personal journey.
C. Inspiration to make positive changes in my life.
D. I'm still figuring out what embracing this energy means for me.

How many did you get - add up the totals

A's	B's	C's	D's

Scoring and Reflection

Mostly A's:
You are deeply in tune with the Pink Moon's energy! Your practice of self-love is robust, and you see every moment as an opportunity for renewal. Keep nurturing your growth and embracing each new beginning.

Mostly B's:
You appreciate the symbolism of the Pink Moon and have a healthy self-care routine. Consider incorporating even more mindful practices to deepen your self-love and balance.

Mostly C's:
You are on a journey of self-discovery. The Pink Moon's energy might serve as a gentle reminder to invest more time in self-reflection and care. Small, consistent steps can lead to significant personal growth.

Mostly D's:
You may feel somewhat disconnected from the ideas of self-love and renewal. The Pink Moon invites you to explore gentle, manageable ways to begin integrating self-care practices into your daily life. Start small - with a short daily meditation or a weekly self-reflection exercise - and allow yourself to grow over time.

If you got mostly A's, smile, give yourself a 'butterfly hug' and move on to the next section on page 53.

If less than all A's reflect on the outcome:
- Is the answer true?
- In what ways could you improve your score?
- Are there any limiting beliefs you need to let go of?
- Could you add a new self-love practice to your life?
  (Examples are on the following page)

Record your reflections on page 52

Practice self-love examples

Take deliberate actions that nurture your mind, body, and soul. Here are some suggestions:

Set Healthy Boundaries - Say no and prioritise your needs. Protect your time and energy by defining what is acceptable in your relationships and commitments.

Mindful Self-Care - Dedicate time to activities that nourish you - whether it is a relaxing bath, a walk in nature, reading a good book, or enjoying your favourite hobby. Put 'Me Days' in your diary and stick to them.

Positive Affirmations - To build a positive internal dialogue, practice speaking kindly to yourself. Write down or recite affirmations like "I am worthy of love and happiness".

Journaling - Keep a journal to reflect on your thoughts and emotions. Writing about your experiences can help you understand your needs, celebrate your progress, and process challenges.

Embrace Your Passions - Engage in activities that make you feel alive and connected. Whether it is art, music, sports, or any other passion, investing in what you love reinforces your sense of identity.

Practice Gratitude - Regularly acknowledge what you appreciate about yourself and your life. Keeping a gratitude journal can shift your focus toward the positive aspects of your journey.

Invest in Personal Growth - Whether through reading, learning new skills, or engaging in therapy, investing time in self-improvement fosters self-respect and confidence.

Each of these practices reinforces the idea that you are worthy of care and attention. Remember, self-love is a journey, not a destination, and every small act of kindness toward yourself adds up to a more balanced and fulfilling life.

Reflections of the self-love quiz

"When you focus on gratitude, everything shifts - your energy, your perspective, and your life."
Dr. Wayne Dyer

Friday 18th April 2025

Cultivating Gratitude
Celebrating Your Achievements

Practical Exercise
Create a Gratitude Jar

You will need
A Mason jar or any decorative jar
Paper or small sticky notes
A pen

-Optional-
Glitter or colourful embellishments
A piece of fabric or string (for decoration)

1. Prepare Your Gratitude Jar
- Find a jar that feels special to you, like a mason jar or any container that resonates with positivity.
- Decorate it using glitter, beads, colorful stickers, or fabric to make it personal and uplifting. I have a key ring on my lock and beads round the outside, as I am not a glitter kind of girl. - Make it personal to you.
- Place the jar somewhere you can see it daily, such as your sacred space, desk, altar, nightstand, or a personal space that you visit often.

2. Set Your Intention for Abundance
- Sit comfortably, close your eyes, and take a few deep breaths.
- As you inhale, visualise the energy of abundance flowing into you. As you exhale, release any feelings of lack or limitation.
- Reflect on what "abundance" means to you—whether it is love, health, joy, opportunities, or wealth.
- Visualise your life blossoming like fruit on a vine, growing more prosperous and fulfilling daily.

3. Write Your First Gratitude Note
- Write down one thing you are grateful for today on a small paper or sticky note.
- It can be big or small—whether it is a moment of kindness, an achievement, or simply the beauty of nature.
- As you write, feel the gratitude within you. Let that feeling of abundance and joy expand in your heart.

5. Practice Daily Gratitude
- Make this a daily habit. Each day, add a note of gratitude to your jar.
- Even on challenging days, find at least one thing to be thankful for.
- By doing this consistently, you train your mind to focus on the positive aspects of your life.

I also like to add things that come to me or remind me of a special day—white feathers, confetti from a birthday or wedding, crystals—the 5 pence pieces!
When I started to write, I was finding 5p's in the oddest places - in sealed envelopes, inside photo frames, in my sock, everywhere I went, a 5p seemed to appear
- so all of these are now in my gratitude jar.

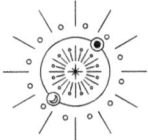

"Spring whispers of possibility and sings of hope. It is the best time to manifest the life you desire."

Unknown

<u>Friday 25th April 2025</u>

Planting the Seeds of Your Dreams
Visualising Your Future

Practical Exercise
Write a letter to your future self

Detailing your life as it will be once your intentions have manifested. Revisit it periodically to remind yourself of the potential you are working toward.

Dear

Friday 2nd May 2025

Grounding and Connection
Rooting Yourself for Growth

Practical Exercise
Barefoot Grounding

This week, set aside 5 minutes daily to stand barefoot on the earth and visualise energy flowing from the earth into your body. This will reinforce your connection with the earth and ground the energy inside you.

Example

| 01 | I stood bare foot on | The grass at the park and felt a connect to the earth | ✓ |

01	I stood bare foot on		☐
02	I stood bare foot on		☐
03	I stood bare foot on		☐
04	I stood bare foot on		☐
05	I stood bare foot on		☐
06	I stood bare foot on		☐
07	I stood bare foot on		☐

Friday 9th May 2025

Planting affirmations for the future

Practical Exercise
Affirmations

Write three affirmations you wish to cultivate and visualise planting them in a garden.

Examples:

- I release old patterns and make room for new growth and possibilities.
- I trust in the natural cycles of life and welcome transformation.
- I am open to the abundance that the Cosmos is offering me.
- With each new day, I am blossoming into my fullest potential.
- I am planting seeds of positivity, and they are flourishing.
- I let go of what no longer serves me and embrace new opportunities.
- I welcome the flow of creativity and inspiration into my life.
- I honour the beauty of new beginnings and trust the process of growth.

Take Action

Look at your Aligned Action lists from pages 32 - 35, pick at least one to follow through on, and then tick it off. The more you get done and tick off, the more dopamine you get. :)

I ticked these off my aligned actions lists

Flower Full Moon
Seeds of New Growth
Sunday 11th May 2025

The full moon energy will give your manifestations a boost, so set aside some time this evening to complete a "New Growth Ritual"

The Flower Moon's name originates from Native Americans, who associated the full moon with the blooming of abundant wildflowers during spring. The name celebrates the natural beauty and renewal of life with the season, marking a time of growth and vibrant energy in nature.

Practical Exercises
Full Moon Release Burn Ritual
Plant Seeds of Abundance
Add fresh flowers to your sacred space/altar

What you will need
Small pieces of paper or flashcards
A pen or pencil
A fireproof container (metal bowl /small hole in the ground)
Matches or a lighter
Crystals, incense, or other spiritual tools to enhance the ritual atmosphere
Plant pots and soil or a space outside in your garden
Seeds that resonate with abundance for you, for example, herbs like basil and mint, which symbolise prosperity, flowers like sunflowers and marigolds, which attract joy and positivity
Water

Meditation
Listen to the "Seeds of Dreams" meditation

Practical Exercise
Full Moon Release Burn Ritual

Harness the powerful energy of the full moon to release fears, doubts, bad habits, or anything that no longer serves you. This ritual helps you let go and make space for new, positive energy. Follow these steps to perform a safe and effective ritual.

Prepare your Space
- Choose a safe outdoor location to burn paper safely, preferably under the full moon's light.

Write
- On separate pieces of paper, write down what you want to release
- Reflect on the fears, doubts, bad habits, or negative energy you wish to release.
- As you write, visualise each issue leaving your mind and heart, transferring onto the paper.

Fold with Intention
- Fold each piece of paper slowly and deliberately.
- As you fold, focus on letting go. Feel the weight of each fear, doubt, or habit begin to lift.
- Channel your intent into the paper, knowing that it will no longer have power over you once burned.

Burn and Release
- Place the folded papers in your fireproof container/ hole in the ground.
- Safely light each paper, one by one, under the full moon.
- Watch as the flames burn the paper, releasing smoke into the night sky.
- Visualise your fears, doubts, and bad habits floating away with the smoke, dissipating into the Cosmos.

Be Mindful and Feel the Release
- As the smoke rises, consciously let go of each burden.
- Feel the joy and lightness of release. Imagine yourself free from negativity, ready to welcome new opportunities.
- Close your ritual with gratitude, thanking the Cosmos and the full moon for their guidance and support.

Safely Conclude the Ritual
- Please make sure the fire is fully extinguished.
- Dispose of the ashes by scattering them in the wind, burying them in the earth, or letting them wash away in water.
- Leave the ritual space with a sense of closure and peace.

"I release what no longer serves me. I let go with gratitude, making space for new blessings to flow. As this flame burns, so does the past, clearing the way for my highest good."

Tee

Practical Exercise
Plant Seeds of Abundance

Just as the Flower Moon celebrates natural beauty, renewal and growth, this task helps you embody that energy by planting 'Seeds of Abundance'. This can be a literal garden, plant pots or a symbolic one through visualisation.

Set Your Intention
- Hold the seeds in your hands and close your eyes.
- Visualise your dreams and goals growing as you nurture these seeds.

Plant with Purpose
- Plant the seeds with love and intention, whispering affirmations like:

"As these seeds grow, so do my dreams and abundance."
"I am open to receiving all the blessings the Cosmos has for me."

Nurture Your Garden
- Water and care for your plants, just as you would your intentions.
- Use this time to practice gratitude and visualise your dreams manifesting.

Celebrate Growth
- As your plants grow and flourish, recognise this as a symbol of your intentions coming to life.
- Acknowledge every little sprout as progress in your journey of manifestation.

Why This Works
- Gratitude raises your vibration, aligning you with the energy of abundance.
- Visualisation activates the brain's dopamine pathways, enhancing motivation and focus.
- Rituals like these create a physical anchor for your intentions, making them more tangible and real.

Friday 16th May 2025

Awakening to Potential
Aligning with Spring's Energy

Practical Exercise
Create a nature walk ritual

Commit to at least a 10-minute walk each day this week. Each time you walk outdoors, pick up something that catches your attention, such as a leaf, stone, or flower. Reflect on what that object symbolises in relation to your intentions or personal growth. Place it in your Sacred Space. Keep a record overleaf.

For Example:
Day 1: You take a 10-minute walk and notice a bright yellow leaf on the ground. You pick it up and reflect on how its colour symbolises change and transition, reminding you to embrace new beginnings. You place it in your Sacred Space as a reminder to welcome change with an open heart.

Day 3: During your walk, you find a small, smooth stone. Holding it in your hand, you feel its solid weight and think about stability and resilience in your life. It represents your strength during challenging times. You place it in your Sacred Space to remind yourself of your inner strength.

Day 5: You come across a delicate flower growing through a crack in the pavement. It symbolises perseverance and beauty in adversity. You take a photo or draw this one as you leave it there to shine bright. But place the photo or drawing in your Sacred Space and reflect on how you, too, can thrive even in difficult situations.

By the end of the week, your Sacred Space holds a collection of meaningful objects, each representing a lesson or insight connected to your personal growth.

01

Today I picked up a _____

This symbolises _____

_____

_____

02

Today I picked up a _____

This symbolises _____

_____

_____

03

Today I picked up a _____

This symbolises _____

_____

_____

04

Today I picked up a _____

This symbolises _____

_____

_____

05
Today I picked up a _____
This symbolises _____
_____
_____

06
Today I picked up a _____
This symbolises _____
_____
_____

07
Today I picked up a _____
This symbolises _____
_____
_____

"In every walk with nature, one receives far more than he seeks."
John Muir

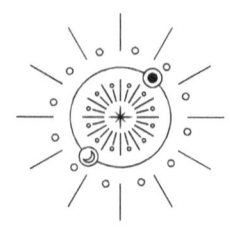

"Reinvent yourself over and over, as many times as it takes to live a life that aligns with your soul."
Unknown

Friday 23rd May 2025

Rebirth of the Self
Cultivating the New You

Practical Exercise
Action Plan

Identify one area of your life that needs the most work - an area that needs to be reinvented (use the Life Wheel on page 21 to help you). Spend this week concentrating on this area, working out an in-depth action plan, and acting on the first step. For example, if you want to change your career, take the first step by researching a course, networking, or updating your CV/resume. If you want to lose weight, look at one food you can give up.

I want to reinvent/change:

My plan of action is:

Friday 30th May 2025

Visualising Success
Envisioning the Life You Desire

Practical Exercise
Visualisation

Spend 10 minutes every day this week practising visualisation. Use your senses - what do you see, feel, hear, and smell in this future version of yourself?

I See

I Smell

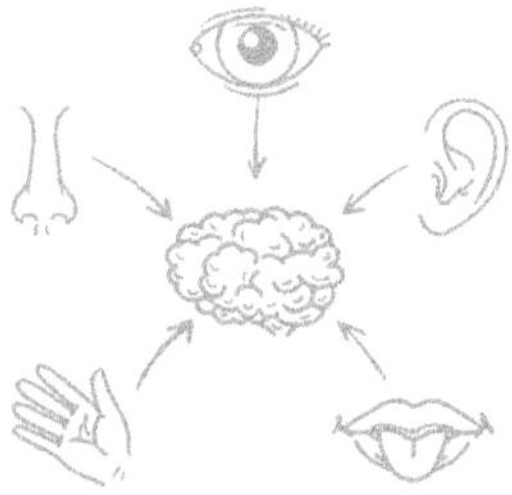

I Hear

I touch

I Taste

Feeling is the most important and hardest part of manifesting because you have to 'feel' what it is like to achieve the goal. So, this week, pay particular attention to how you will feel once you achieve your intention. And try to actually feel the feeling.

I Feel

Friday 6th June 2025

Visualising Success
Map Out The Life You Desire

Practical Exercise
Create a Mind Map

Using the notes from last week where you used all your senses, create a Mind Map, including any adjustments from your Vision Board. You can create one overall 'Mind Map' for all your intentions for the year or one for each.

- To create a mind map, start with a circle in the centre of the paper - this is your overall goal.
- Then, draw sub-branchs off and clearly label them.
- Then, draw sub-branches off that and break it down into smaller ideas, categories, or related concepts.
- Use colours, symbols, or images to clarify connections and enhance memory retention.
- Keep the structure flexible, allowing new ideas to be added as they arise.
- This visual approach helps organise thoughts, making complex information easier to understand and recall.

Why This Works
Studies on goal-setting theory suggest that breaking larger resolutions into smaller, realistic steps increases dopamine (the brain's reward chemical), reinforcing positive behaviour and making it easier to stick to new habits.

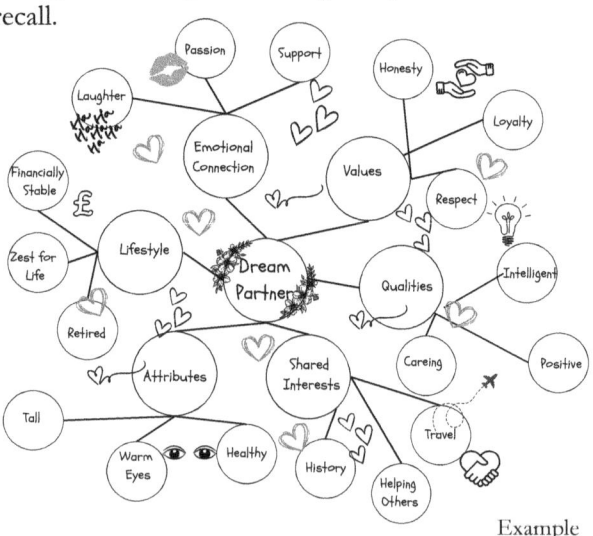

Example

Strawberry Full Moon
Balancing Light and Shadow
Tuesday 10th June 2025

The name "Strawberry Moon" comes from Native Americans, who linked it to the strawberry harvest in North America. Specifically, the Algonquin tribes used this term to signal the time for picking strawberries. It is a beautiful reminder of nature's rhythms and the rich harvests that come with the season.

Practical Exercises
Self Assessment Quiz - Identify Limiting Beliefs
Re-framing Limiting Beliefs
Nurturing Your Intentions and Creating Action Plans
Add something red, ie red flowers or Jasper, to your scared space/altar

Meditation
Listen to the "Strawberry Moon Nurturing your Intentions" meditation

"Intuition is but the whisper of your soul. The more you listen, the louder it gets."

Tee

Practical Exercise
Self-Assessment Quiz

This quiz will help you uncover limiting beliefs that may be holding you back in different areas of your life. Be honest with your answers, as self-awareness is the first step toward growth.

Instructions
For each statement, rate how much you agree or disagree on a scale of 1 to 5:
1 = Strongly Disagree | 2 = Disagree | 3 = Neutral | 4 = Agree | 5 = Strongly Agree

Part 1: Self-Worth
1. I often doubt my ability to succeed in new situations.
2. I feel like I am not as capable as others in achieving my goals.
3. I struggle to accept compliments or recognition from others.
4. I believe my value is tied to what I achieve or produce.
5. I often think I am not good enough to deserve success or happiness.

Part 2: Relationships
6. I believe people will only like me if I meet certain expectations.
7. I am afraid of being abandoned if I express my true feelings or needs.
8. I feel like I need to give more than I receive to maintain relationships.
9. I often think others' happiness is more important than my own.
10. I feel unworthy of love or acceptance just as I am.

Instructions

For each statement, rate how much you agree or disagree on a scale of 1 to 5:
1 = Strongly Disagree | 2 = Disagree | 3 = Neutral | 4 = Agree | 5 = Strongly Agree

Part 3: Money and Abundance

☐ 11. I believe making a lot of money requires hard work and sacrifice.
☐ 12. I think people who are wealthy are often greedy or selfish.
☐ 13. I feel uncomfortable asking for what I am worth in financial or work-related situations.
☐ 14. I think there is not enough success or wealth to go around.
☐ 15. I often worry about running out of money, even when I am financially secure.

Part 4: Personal Growth and Goals

☐ 16. I am afraid to take risks because I might fail.
☐ 17. I believe it is safer to stay in my comfort zone than to try something new.
☐ 18. I think I need to be perfect before I can start pursuing my goals.
☐ 19. I often compare myself to others and feel inadequate.
☐ 20. I think success is something that happens to others, not to me.

> *"I am aligned with the energy of spring, attracting peace and prosperity."*
>
> — Tee

Score Guide

Add up your scores for each section, then total all your scores: 0–20 Points (Per section):

0–10: Few limiting beliefs in this area.
11–15: Some limiting beliefs that might occasionally hold you back.
16–20: Significant limiting beliefs that could be affecting your life.

Total Points

80–100: Limiting beliefs are likely playing a significant role in your life.
60–79: You may have moderate limiting beliefs in certain areas.
40–59: Some limiting beliefs are present but not dominant.
20–39: Though occasional doubts may arise, you have minimal limiting belief

 Interpreting Your Results

1. High Scores in Specific Areas: Focus on addressing the limiting beliefs in those areas (e.g., relationships, money).

2. High Total Score: This may indicate a general pattern of self-doubt or negative thinking that could benefit from mindfulness, coaching, or therapy.

3. Low Scores: You are likely aligned with empowering beliefs, but periodic reflection can help maintain this balance.

 Putting it all together

Take your scores and work through the exercise on the following pages to learn how to identify your limiting beliefs, reframe them, and then take aligned action to let them go. Please do not worry if you can only do one to two at this stage.

Identify Your Limiting Beliefs - Reflect on the highest-scoring statements and write them down.

Challenge Them - Ask, "Is this belief absolutely true?" and "What evidence contradicts this belief?"

Reframe - Replace limiting beliefs with empowering ones. For example, change "I am not good enough" to "I am capable and worthy." Detailed examples of this can be found in the main book, 'Unlock Your Cosmic Flow'

Take Action - Test new beliefs by taking small, aligned actions that challenge your doubts.

I have a Limiting Belief of:

_____

Is this belief absolutely true? _____

What evidence contradicts this belief? _____

_____

Re-frame - Write an empowering belief here that counterbalances the one above. For example, change "I am not good enough" to "I am capable and worthy."

_____

_____

Take Action - Test this new belief by taking small, aligned actions that challenge your doubts. I plan to take the following actions:

_____

_____

 I have a Limiting Belief of:

_____

Is this belief absolutely true? _____

What evidence contradicts this belief? _____

_____

Re-frame - Write an empowering belief here that counterbalances the one above. For example, change "I am not good enough" to "I am capable and worthy."

_____

_____

Take Action - Test this new belief by taking small, aligned actions that challenge your doubts. I plan to take the following actions:

_____

_____

I have a Limiting Belief of:

Is this belief absolutely true?

What evidence contradicts this belief?

Re-frame - Write an empowering belief here that counterbalances the one above. For example, change "I am not good enough" to "I am capable and worthy."

Take Action - Test this new belief by taking small, aligned actions that challenge your doubts. I plan to take the following actions:

I have a Limiting Belief of:

Is this belief absolutely true?

What evidence contradicts this belief?

Re-frame - Write an empowering belief here that counterbalances the one above. For example, change "I am not good enough" to "I am capable and worthy."

Take Action - Test this new belief by taking small, aligned actions that challenge your doubts. I plan to take the following actions:

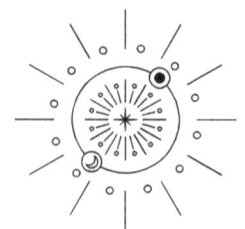

"The only limits you have are the ones you believe."
Wayne Dyer

Friday 13th June 2025

Refining Intentions
Progress, Setbacks and Feelings

Practical Exercise
Intention review

- Look back at your Intentions from page 21 and adjust them as needed.

- Use the pages overleaf to write down any progress, setbacks, and feelings related to your Intentions.

- Then, refine your Action Plan.

Why this is important: As we grow, we gain more knowledge and understanding, and with that, our life goals can change. So we should always reflect back enough to bring any changes into the now so we can manifest for the future with full intent.

"Every setback is a setup for a comeback. Trust the journey, embrace the lessons, and rise stronger than before."
Unknown

I WANT
TO MANIFEST

PROGRESS SO FAR

SET BACKS

MY ACTION PLAN - TO DO LIST

HOW I AM FEELING ABOUT THIS INTENTION

I WANT TO MANIFEST

PROGRESS SO FAR

SET BACKS

MY ACTION PLAN - TO DO LIST

HOW I AM FEELING ABOUT THIS INTENTION

I WANT
TO MANIFEST

PROGRESS SO FAR

SET BACKS

MY ACTION PLAN - TO DO LIST

HOW I AM FEELING ABOUT THIS INTENTION

I WANT TO MANIFEST

PROGRESS SO FAR

SET BACKS

MY ACTION PLAN - TO DO LIST

HOW I AM FEELING ABOUT THIS INTENTION

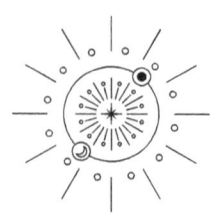

"The more grateful you are, the more present you become, and the more joy you bring into your life."

Louise Hay

Friday 20th June 2025

Gratitude Jar
Refection

Practical Exercise
Gratitude Jar Review

Gratitude Jar Review

- Sit down with your Gratitude Jar.
- Take out all the notes and read them aloud, reflecting on the blessings you have received.
- Light a pink or red candle to amplify the energy of gratitude, love, and abundance.
- Spend a few moments in reflection, allowing the feeling of gratitude to wash over you.
- Place the notes back into the jar with care. Place the jar in your sacred place or anywhere that feels meaningful to you, and you will see it every day.
- This jar becomes a visual reminder of the abundance present in your life, reinforcing the energy of gratitude and positivity.

You do not need to make this a daily ritual anymore, but I love adding to mine on special days and celebration moments - the highs, the good days, and the memorable occasions. As a family, we have done this for years and open the jar on the Georgian Calendar New Year as the year date changes - which is right in the depths of winter - and read aloud all the cherished memories and achievements from the year. It is a beautiful way to relive joy and gratitude.

I also find it incredibly uplifting on difficult days. Whenever I am feeling down, I pick a note from the jar, and it instantly lifts my spirits, reminding me of the good times and the blessings I have experienced.

Practical Exercise
Life Wheel Refection

Create a new Life Wheel and compare it to the last one on page 19.

How It Works - Reminder
The Life Wheel is typically a circle divided into segments, each representing a different aspect of life. You rate your satisfaction in each area on a scale from 1 to 10, then plot these scores on the wheel. The result shows whether your life feels balanced or if some areas need more attention and the progress you have made since the start of Spring.

Common Life Areas in a Life Wheel
Though categories can be customised, a standard Life Wheel often includes:

- Career and Work – Job satisfaction, growth, and fulfilment.
- Finances – Stability, income, and financial security.
- Health and Wellness – Physical and mental well-being.
- Personal Growth – Learning, self-improvement, and mindset.
- Relationships – Love, friendships, and family connections.
- Spirituality – Inner peace, faith, or connection to a higher purpose.
- Fun and Recreation – Hobbies, leisure, and joy.
- Environment – Living space, work environment, and surroundings.

What to do
- Contemplate each key area of life and rate it on a scale of 1 - 10. 1 being totally dissatisfied and 10 being totally satisfied and content.
- Then, draw a line around the arc or colour in the section from the centre towards the outer circle for each key area.
- Then compare this wheel with the one you did on page 19.

Life Wheel

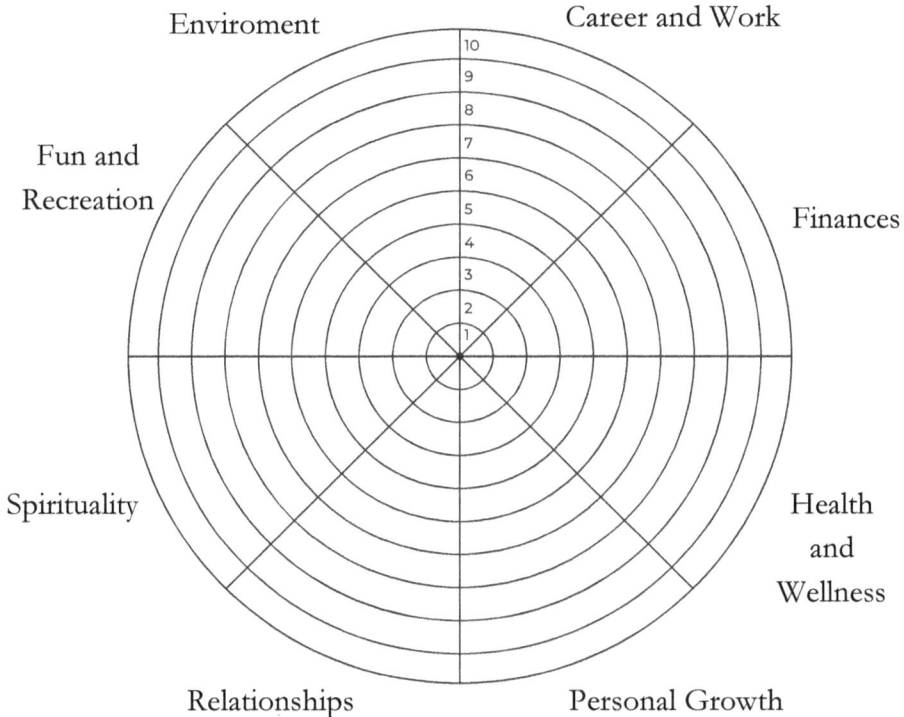

What areas of my life have improved?

What areas of my life have got more out of balance?

Reflect on these and try to work out why these changes have occurred.

What steps would you like to put in place to balance this wheel?

Celebrate a Win
Many small shifts, add up to big changes

Use the Gratitude Jar, the Life Wheel and all the ticks on your Action Plans to reflect on the progress you have made during spring - even the smallest actions count - sending an application, updating your CV/resume, networking, or simply believing in yourself a little more today than yesterday. Take a moment to celebrate your efforts rather than dwelling on what has not happened yet. We are in spring and only just sowing the seeds of change. Obviously, if you have achieved one of your intentions, celebrate, celebrate, celebrate and thank the Cosmos for working with you.

If not much has changed, remember that transformation is not always instant, and progress does not always arrive in bold, dramatic leaps. Sometimes, small shifts - the slight change in mindset, the extra bit of effort, the willingness to try again build up over time to create something extraordinary. Even if you do not see the results you expected by now, it does not mean that nothing is happening.

Every choice you make in alignment with your vision is planting a seed, even if you cannot see the roots forming beneath the surface.

However, looking inward with radical honesty is worth it if progress feels stagnant. Are your dominant thoughts supporting your goals, or are they quietly working against them? It is one thing to say, "I want a new career," but if the more profound, more persistent belief is "I'm not good at learning new things," your energy is sending mixed signals. Acknowledging this is where the real work happens - examining self-sabotage, rewriting limiting beliefs, and aligning your thoughts with your desires. We will look at this in more depth in the Summer Workbook.

Remember, the energy you feed grows. If you nurture self-doubt, it will expand. But if you focus on appreciation, momentum, and belief, those will flourish instead.

If you feel this is you, look back at your Action Plan, and if you have only ticked one box, celebrate that, for that is progress. Keep a record overleaf as a reminder of your wins so far.

My Wins To Date

My achievement(s) is/are

My reward is:

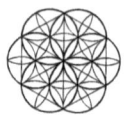

Embracing Spring's gifts as we move into Summer

As Spring draws to a close, it leaves behind the gifts of renewal, growth, and fresh beginnings. This season of awakening has invited you to plant seeds of intention, nurture your dreams, and align with the vibrant energy of possibility. Just as the earth has blossomed with life, so too have your goals and aspirations begun to take root.

As you transition into summer, you carry the momentum and optimism cultivated during Spring. Summer invites you to take inspired action, nurture what you have planted, and fully embrace the energy of expansion and vitality. It is a time to celebrate growth, harness the sun's power, and step confidently into your manifestations.

Honor life's cyclical nature and trust the growth and transformation process. Spring has given you the vision; now, summer encourages you to bring that vision to full bloom. With gratitude for Spring's renewal, step forward into the next chapter, ready to nurture your dreams with purpose and passion.

Carry the spirit of Spring's awakening with you, allowing your intentions to flourish under the vibrant light of summer. Just as nature continues its growth journey, so do you move forward, aligned with the rhythms of the earth and the unfolding of your highest potential.

*"The seeds planted in spring,
will be nurtured in Summer
as I am renewed, refreshed,
and ready to blossom"*

Tee

About the author

Teanna Taylor is a compassionate spiritual energy coach and meditation facilitator, as well as the co-founder of Energy Flows and Rainbow Breath Kids. With a heartfelt commitment to helping others tap into their inner strength, she also established Migraine Talk, a supportive platform for those navigating the challenges of chronic migraines.

Her story has resonated with many and has been featured in national magazines and newspapers. She has also shared her experiences on an international stage as a guest speaker at global pharmaceutical conferences and has facilitated meditation for over 14,000 people worldwide. Teanna has touched countless lives.

Teanna's journey took a transformative turn from a city career when she faced a minor stroke and endured a ten-year struggle with a debilitating migraine. Yes, one migraine 24/7 for a decade! She discovered the deep connection between mind, body, and energy through the many silent days and meditations. Combining scientific insights with ancient wisdom, she now empowers others through evidence-based techniques from neurology, psychology, quantum physics, and cherished spiritual traditions.

Residing in Whitstable, UK, with her four children, Teanna continues her heartfelt mission to help others heal, awaken, and unlock their highest potential. She understands the difficulties many face and is dedicated to guiding them on their paths to wellness and self-discovery.

Also available by Teanna Taylor

Unlock Your Cosmic Flow
Manifest Your Dreams in Harmony with Nature's Rhymes

Cosmic Flow - Summer Workbook
Cosmic Flow - Autumn Workbook
Cosmic Flow - Winter Workbook

www.TeannaTaylor.com

www.ingramcontent.com/pod-product-compliance
Lightning Source LLC
Chambersburg PA
CBHW041309110526
44590CB00028B/4296